DANGER
in the sky
Narrow Escapes in the Air

John Townsend

Published in association with The Basic Skills Agency

Hodder & Stoughton

A MEMBER OF THE HODDER HEADLINE GROUP

Acknowledgements
Cover artwork: Fred Van Deelan
Illustration: Josephine Blake
Photos: pp. iv, 5, 8, 25, 28 © Corbis; p. 11 © Quadrant Picture Library

Orders: please contact Bookpoint Ltd, 130 Milton Park, Abingdon, Oxon OX14 4SB.
Telephone: (44) 01235 827720, Fax: (44) 01235 400454. Lines are open from 9.00 – 6.00,
Monday to Saturday, with a 24 hour message answering service. Email address:
orders@bookpoint.co.uk

British Library Cataloguing in Publication Data
A catalogue record for this title is available from The British Library

ISBN 0 340 84860 X

First published 2002
Impression number   10 9 8 7 6 5 4 3 2 1
Year   2007 2006 2005 2004 2003 2002

Typeset by SX Composing DTP, Rayleigh, Essex.
Printed in Great Britain for Hodder & Stoughton Educational, a division of Hodder
Headline Plc, 338 Euston Road, London NW1 3BH by Bath Press Ltd.

Contents

As free as a bird . . . but would *you* risk hang-gliding?

1   What Goes Up . . .

You never know what's going on up in the clouds.
There are narrow escapes in the sky all the time.
Near misses seem to happen in mid-air most days.

The sky has always held great mystery.
Old myths and legends told of strange things
falling to earth.
There was great fear of the unknown
in the world above.
Just what was beyond those clouds?
No one had any idea.

It was only when we began to fly
that we felt in control of the skies.
Over the last hundred years, we have really
taken off. But are we as clever as the birds?
Some stories may make you wonder.
Some are too scary to believe.

They say, 'what goes up must come down'.
But it's the coming down that can be the problem.
That's when danger can strike.
The sky holds many surprises –
with some of them not very far off the ground . . .
too close for comfort.

These true stories from the last few years
may make you look up more often.
After all, we never know what may happen next
just above our heads.
So start looking up now!

2   A Plunge to Earth

Jumping from a plane with a parachute
is as close to free flying as you can get.
Sky-diving is high on thrills.
But now and again things can go wrong.

Dave Clements had jumped hundreds of times.
In November 2000, he jumped
from a plane over Coventry.
But things went wrong.
He fell 700 metres at a speed of 150 miles per hour.
His parachute didn't open.

He said, 'I spun round and round.
It was like being in a tumble drier.
I had no control at all.'
He fell like a stone.
With seconds to go before he hit the ground,
he pulled the cord again.

The chute began to open but it was too late.
It was tangled. He knew he didn't stand a chance.

The crowd saw Dave plunge towards an
aircraft hangar.
He crashed with a thud onto the iron roof.
It dented but broke his fall.
He lay very still.
He only broke an arm and a few ribs.
He couldn't believe he was still alive.

Not many survive a fall like that.
It was an amazing escape.
Dave lived to jump another day.

Sky-diving – high on thrills or high on risks?

3   Sucked Out

In June 1990, British Airways flight 5390
hit the headlines.
It was just another holiday flight
from Birmingham to Malaga.
It was nearly a disaster.

The cockpit's six windows were new.
Just after take-off, at 800 metres above Oxford,
there was a loud crack.
One of the new windows blew out.
Air rushed out of the plane.

The captain held on to the controls
but it was no good.
He was sucked out of his seat.
He slid under his safety belt
as he tried to cling on for dear life.
But the air hissed past him,
sucking him to the gap at the window.

He slipped through the hole
out on to the plane's nose-cone.

Two stewards dived to grab the captain.
They held his feet and tried to pull him back in.
But they were nearly sucked out, too.
They had to strap themselves down.
They pulled and pulled
but couldn't get the captain back in the cockpit.

There were 81 shocked passengers on board.
The plane dived and lost pressure.
The air dropped to minus 20 degrees.
The co-pilot grabbed an oxygen mask
and took the controls.
He called to air control.
He had to make an emergency landing.

He had to land the plane on his own
at Southampton, 15 minutes later.
The captain was still hanging by his feet
from the window.
Blood and bits of his shirt were frozen
to the nose-cone.

People on the ground must have stared in shock
as the plane came to a halt.

All the passengers were fine. The crew was stunned.
The captain was hurt but he survived.
He had frostbite and a broken arm.
It had been a close shave.
Yet another near miss up in the clouds.

This is your captain speaking . . . help!

4   Terror in the Clouds

Taff worked for the Royal Air Force.
He mended planes.
Pilots let him know if anything needed fixing.
He was always happy to take a look at the engines.
Although he couldn't fly aircraft,
he knew all about how they worked.

He was asked to take a look at a jet.
It had a small fault with one of the dials
in the cockpit.
It would just be a short job – or so he thought.
Taff climbed into the plane to see
if he could find what was wrong.
It would need a quick trip along the runway
for him to see how the engine ran.
He had done this sort of thing many times.
Taff would give the jet a good test.
It didn't need to fly for that.
He would drive it fast along the runway
and slam on the brakes.

It was an easy way to tell what needed to be done.

The plane was a 1500 miles-per-hour
Lightning F1 Jet.
In those days it was one of the
fastest aircraft in the world.
It was the pride of the RAF.
Taff looked at all the dials, switches
and wires in the cockpit.
There were rows of lights and numbers.
A pilot had to know what they all meant.
He was glad he wasn't a pilot!

Taff needed to try out the
throttle levers and the brakes.
They would show him what was wrong
with the faulty dial. He could soon sort that out.
Taff started the engines.
They blasted with an ear-splitting roar.
He slowly opened the throttle
and the aircraft moved down the runway.
The great engines burst with power and noise.
As Taff let off the brakes,
the jet sped along the runway with a loud scream.

The Lightning F1 Jet – not for learner drivers!

After a short burst of speed,
Taff slammed on the brakes.
He watched the dial as the jet came to a halt.
He took out his note pad and
wrote down the reading from the dial.
He would need to do this one more time.
He turned the jet round and got ready
to give it one more quick roar down the runway.

Once again, Taff sent the jet
bursting along the tarmac.
He shot past other planes parked near their hangars.
He got ready to slam on the brakes.
There was a sudden loud bang
and flames flashed from the tail pipes.
The brakes went dead . . .
as the jet kept gaining speed.

In shock, Taff tried to shut down the engines.
Nothing. The jet thrust on, faster and faster.
A fuel tanker was on the runway just ahead.
He was shooting towards it
but he just couldn't slow down the jet.
He flashed right past,
missing the tanker by a few metres.

Taff was now racing along at lift-off speed . . .
towards the end of the runway.
There were houses not far beyond.
All he could do now was take off!
He had to think fast.
What did he have to do
to get this jet off the ground?
There were many switches in front of him
but none of them made sense to him.
He pulled back a lever and
the jet rose up in the air with a scream.

The jet was in the sky – shooting up like a rocket.
Below him, Taff saw his friends like dots –
running round in panic.
There was nothing they could do.
He was on his own up there at the controls of a jet
that took months of training to fly!

Taff had to keep close to the airfield
or he'd be lost forever.
Five hundred metres below him,
they were on red alert.
The fire engines were ready on the runway
as he pushed on one of the pedals.

The jet began to turn to the left.
Taff was certain he was about to crash.
His life flashed before him.
At least he'd die fast – in a ball of flame.
But he wouldn't go without a fight.
He would try to land this machine –
if it was the last thing he did.
His hands shook as they grabbed the controls.
Down . . . down . . . down . . .
left a bit . . . too fast . . . too high.
He pulled the jet up into the sky again
and turned back to try again.
Death could only be seconds away.

He would try once more to get down in one piece.
He made sure the houses were behind him.
He would crash into the woods.
The jet began to bank round. It was now or never.
The runway was just ahead – rushing up to him.

The nose began to drop. The jet gave a jolt.
The wheels hit the runway.
He was down . . . but still going much too fast.
Taff pulled with all his strength on the brake lever.
Rubber burned. Smoke rose and sparks flew.

At last he began to slow down.

Just ten minutes after shooting up into the sky,

Taff came to a halt at the end of the runway.

Just a few metres more

and he would have smashed into the trees.

He couldn't believe his luck.

His feet touched the ground.

He was back in one piece.

Back from his brush with death in the sky.

5   Swooping and Diving

It was April in 1993 when Steve Clark fell to earth.
He was flying a hang-glider in Essex.
The fields were far below him . . .
until he hit the wires.

Steve crashed into power lines.
His glider's metal frame struck the cables –
and 275,000 volts.
He spun off the wires with a crack –
only to hit more cables.
There was a crackle, a fizz and a shower of sparks.
The glider fell 50 metres to the ground.

Luckily for Steve, he didn't touch both lines
at the same time.
If he had, there wouldn't be much left of him
or his glider. Nor the pylons!
He went to hospital but lived to fly
his hang-glider again.

In New Zealand in 1992, someone else had a
narrow escape.
This time it was with a small plane.
Maurie sat on the tail of the plane.
It began to taxi along a beach.

Maurie must have been too heavy because
the plane's nose rose up too high.
The wind got under the wings
and the plane took off.
The pilot had to open the throttle
to stop the engine from cutting out.
The plane began to bank round over the sea.
Maurie clung on for his life.
If he moved, the plane might tip.
But he was holding on to the rudder
so the pilot couldn't steer.
Maurie tried to pull himself along the plane
but this sent it in a spin.
A wing dipped and hit the sea.
He was flung off into the sea
as the plane crashed into the water.

Both Maurie and the pilot had a lucky escape.
They both swam away from the wreck.
The plane never flew again!

6 Mr Bean in a Spin

Many stories tell of people who have flown
light aircraft in a panic.
Not because there was anything wrong with the plane.
Nor because the weather was bad or the sky was dark.

What could be your worst fear?
You are in a plane looking down at the view.
One minute it's all very calm.
The next minute you have to leap into the cockpit.
The pilot has passed out and you are now in control.
You have never flown a plane before.
What do you do?
What a nightmare!

It happened in 2001 to the actor who plays Mr Bean. The pilot of a small plane passed out over Kenya. Newspapers told the story:

Rowan Atkinson, who plays Mr Bean, had to grab the controls of a private plane in the African skies. He and his family were on holiday in Kenya. The family of four was flying over the game reserves when their pilot suddenly fainted.

Atkinson climbed into the front of the plane and tried to work out what to do. The light aircraft shook from side to side then started to nose-dive. His wife tried to revive the pilot, who woke up after a few minutes. He got back at the controls and was able to land the plane safely. It was almost a 'Mr Has-Been' for Mr Bean!

So next time you take a flight, it might be a good idea to brush up on your pilot's licence first!

7   The Eagle has Landed

Some horror stories in the sky are far-fetched.
There are many myths about birds of prey swooping
down and carrying away babies . . .
but some seem to be true.
In fact some victims have lived to tell the tale.

Large eagles can carry off young deer weighing
15 kilograms.
So can a bird really grab a human baby?
Could anyone survive the sharp talons of an eagle?

One of the Scottish islands has a story from 1790.
A young couple were helping with the harvest
while their baby girl was at the edge of the field.

There was suddenly a loud flapping in the hedge.
The farm workers looked in horror.
A large sea eagle held the baby in its talons.

They all ran at it but it flew off,
still gripping the baby.
They saw it fly out over the sea.
Its wings skimmed the waves.
The baby's mother screamed.

The eagle rose over some rocky islands.
Everyone knew there were eagle nests there.
Some men ran to the shore and got into a boat.
They rowed over 3 miles to the island.
They saw a nest high up on a cliff.
As they got near, they saw
the baby being pecked by young eagles.

A boy who lived on the island
climbed up to the nest.
He held the baby in his arms
and was able to carry her down the cliff.
She was safe.

The story tells that when the baby grew up,
she married the boy who saved her.
Their offspring still live there today.
However, the eagles must have
flown the nest by now!

8   Just Scratched

The jet flew across the Essex sky with a roar.
It flashed through the air at 250 miles per hour.
Tom Maloney had his younger brother Des
with him in the cockpit.
He showed Des what it was like to fly upside down.
It was 1994.

Twenty-eight year old Des
felt the speed and power of the engines.
But then he felt something else –
as the ejector seat fired for no reason.
In seconds, he shot out into the air
1000 metres above the ground.
As he fell to earth, the jet roared on.
His parachute began to open – almost.
The cords wrapped round his neck
and he landed in a heap in a field.

As he lay there, still stunned,
a boy came up to him and said,
'Can I have your parachute?'
Des looked round to see people staring.
He was just outside a supermarket near Colchester!

Meanwhile, Tom landed the jet 20 miles away.
He had no idea where his brother was.
Des went to hospital but he wasn't badly hurt.
He was certainly lucky.
He must have been one of
the supermarket's special offers!

9   Who'd have Thought it?

Humans have always tried to be like the birds.
The sky is the place to be.
But now and again the birds might want
the sky to themselves.
They tell us it belongs to them.

Danger in the sky comes in many forms.
Sometimes it has feathers and a beak.
They attack from above!

In 2001, there were two stories
about these kinds of attacks.
Both show how birds can swoop down from the
clouds and take us by surprise.

The newspapers put it like this:

JOGGER BUZZED BY BUZZARD

Simon Harvey, 27, was out on an early morning run in the Lake District. A large buzzard swept down at a speed of 80 mph. It struck him on the head with such force he fell to the ground. As Simon tried to get away, the bird of prey dived again. It lashed out with its beak and claws. He was soon covered in blood. The bird flew off and left him in a real mess. A man who found him said, "I thought he'd been hit by a car." Simon was treated in hospital for 15 wounds to the head.

Have you heard about the bird
that stopped the mail?
The postman was too scared to do his rounds.

And where did this terror of the skies strike?
Africa? Hill country? The jungle?
No, in the middle of London!

A seagull stops London letters (except air mail!)

SEAGULL STOPS THE MAIL

A dive-bombing seagull has scared away the postman in a London street near Regents Park. The
Royal Mail told local people it was unsafe for
their post to be delivered. The seagull was seen as
a danger to anyone walking along the street.
Attacks by animals cost The Royal Mail £1 mil-
lion a year!

10 High Thoughts

From the earliest of times people longed to fly.
They dreamed of getting into the air somehow.

The old Greek story told of Icarus and his father.
They tried to fly like the birds
using wax wings and feathers.
But Icarus flew too near the sun.
He got too hot and the wax on his wings melted.
He fell into the sea.
Perhaps this story still has a message.
Some people say, 'The sky's the limit!'

'The sky's the limit': but Icarus went too high.

In other words, there's no end
to how high they want to go.
But they forget the danger up there.
Maybe all of these stories remind us of
Icarus trying to fly.
The sky can be a scary place.
And the higher we fly, the further it is to fall!